D1409067

DEDICATION

Rush Limbaugh.
May you rest in peace knowing you did more than
your share!

Ken Osborne.
My friend, mentor, and supporter, no matter what!

Last, but really first, my wife Nancy.
Who had the courage to let me stay the course.

Special Thanks to my good friend, **Mel Kelley** who worked tirelessly to edit this work. And, to everyone else that contributed their talents.

Table of Contents

Prologue: 2

What's Going On?   7

Are White People Inherently Racist?   12

Blind Rage and Misdirection: 29

America's Enemies: 36

How it all Began: 41

30,000 Foot View: 51

Why This Essay?   54

China: 63

China is not our friend: 68

Other Bad Actors plus Attacks on Capitalism and
    Individualism: 78

Can We Win? And Who is John Galt?"   83

Winning this Battle Requires Three Things: 89

Why the Second Amendment is the last line
of defense: 94

The Question of: "Can Voting Force an End of
    America As We Know It?   101

Prologue:

In the latter half of the 20th century, the United States of America was the undisputed, most powerful force for good in the world and the lone remaining superpower. A nation that enshrined the concept of personal freedom and liberty above all else and the personal responsibility that comes with it as our primary core value. Our power and strength were enshrined in "**The United States Constitution**" which guaranteed the concept of Individual Liberty, Freedom, and Rights. We used that freedom to create the greatest economic and social miracle the world has ever known. We were the nation that stood in the breach against Hitler, Mao, and Stalin among others, and created the Engine of the World. Seemingly out of nowhere a dystopian/Orwellian view developed amongst a surprising number of its citizens. That position directly attempts to refute the truth of how this miracle was achieved and the philosophies and actions that made it possible. The very legitimacy of the nation has been challenged.

As you read along, it is important to resist a feeling of despair. Despair that so many of us feel personally and profoundly as the rug was pulled out from under us last November. It became clear that Democrats were spring-loaded for this opportunity, that they created through an unprecedented election. Elections have consequences we have all heard. We are going to tell a complex story here. It's depressing in its enormity and scope, the dedication of its leaders, and the ends they seek to achieve. Yet, we will beat them in the end, just as we have beaten all the others that have challenged American Exceptionalism in the past. We are the Engine of the World and where the finest minds come to live and prosper. Within the millions of dedicated capitalists and conservatives will come, leaders, thinkers, and even soldiers. As Shawn Hannity likes to say "Let not your heart be troubled." In the end, we will succeed. Let's read on, we've got a lot to discuss.

While the end of the story is by no means yet in sight; tens of millions of supposed American citizens are cheering on what we will call **The Darkness**. The ultimate goal of this Darkness is not to see everyone be equal, but rather that everyone is made equally poor and subservient to the State. Some call this Equity. I call it Hell on Earth with the supremacy of the Federal government over the individual, a dramatic snuffing out of individualism. An active movement exists that has as a central goal, to pull down, to destroy, and to burden productive and independent thinking people. In the past, efforts and beliefs centered on lifting society as a whole. Some believe the Pizza only has 8 pieces and can't have more. Conservatives believe the pie can be, has been grown to meet the demand. This is a principal difference between the two sides today.

We used to call that Communism; today it's Progressive. How to explain how this Black Hole seemingly developed out of nowhere, and that everything we knew, everything that was good and special about America has now become distorted, perverted, and vilified by a minority of its citizenry? Yet few push back. Why?

The answer is neither simple nor obvious. Enemies of the People wearing the proverbial Emperor's Clothes over two generations, sharpened their tactics, created alliances, and most importantly, found the right issue(s) that could pierce every layer of protection the Republic had devised to defend and maintain itself. The Story is insidious, ugly, and true. America's enemies are dedicated to its destruction. Like my father always taught me, America plays Checkers, our enemies play Chess.

An important point to understand is this story is not fundamentally about race. It is a story about subversion and sleight of hand. It is a classic story of manipulating people while employing hidden motives and keeping those methods hidden. Watch carefully, but always keep in mind that magicians understand the art of misdirection very well. What you see is very definitely not necessarily what is going on, nor are you seeing the truth, the underlying truth. Now, let's use a bit of that critical thinking that as human beings God has bestowed upon us, but as in all things, we must choose to employ it as we navigate life.

What we will attempt to do in this essay is to define the enemy, give you a sense of why they are doing this, and the strategy and tactics they employ to win. We will highlight the improbability of it all, but demonstrate that an intractable enemy utilizing mental Jitsu has successfully shaken us to our core. If we do not meet the challenge, America, we are lost.

The Darkness we face is mentally debilitating and exhausting. All is not lost, do not lose hope. Ultimately, this essay is about the way back. This document does not sugarcoat the challenges and facts on the ground. I hope that your takeaway is that there is hope and that you are not alone. Together, we will face the enemy and defeat them. How we do it and how long it will take are not known today; that's tactics. In time, we will figure that out. However, strategically, we will come to understand the enemy and that they must be defeated. That's a major first step. Please read along as we discuss a much larger picture than you might at first be prepared to believe could possibly exist.

Chapter One

What's Going On?

Do you feel that you may be one of the millions tarred with the brush of what's called "White Privilege?"

First, what is White Privilege? According to **Suffolk University**, the Definition of White Privilege "is the concrete benefits of access to resources and social rewards and the power to share the norms and values of a society that Whites receive, tacitly or explicitly, by their position in a racist society."

Uber Liberals and Progressives in general, echo President Obama's preposterous claim, agree that "You did not build that " is true. What is not said but implied here is the implication that all work is of equal value and that no one should think of themselves better than the next man. As a consequence, and therefore, all outcomes should be equal or nearly so. The takeaway here is that success is societal and should never be ascribed to someone personally. Everyone owes "The State for their start and any positive outcome that ensues cannot be attributed to you, but instead that of the State."

The natural extension of this line of thinking that success is not yours to claim is also the corollary that individual failures are not yours either. This is an attack on the very basis of America, where individual responsibility is the nexus from which every other right flows. You can't have one without the other. In essence, for success to be achieved, some will naturally fail.

In their view, if a Black person strives and succeeds, it's because the State empowered him/her. The same logic holds that black success is not an individual success, but a borrowing of societies, which can be taken away at a moment's notice, should it be beneficial to the State. If a White person succeeds, it's never due to their initiative either. At best, it's the State and at worst, it's White Privilege that is responsible for that success.

Big Business is in many ways an extension of the State. Two entities, but very similar in their aims, make-ups, and aspirations. There exists a revolving door between business and government. Big business started the concept of Trans Nationalism in this country. Let's explain. If companies are not fundamentally loyal to their home countries, they naturally become strong adherents of "Open Borders". If a government employee leaves government and works for Big Business or if it works the other way around, what would you expect? Loyalty and self-interest are the shared aims of Big Business and Government. Loyalty is to fellow workers and to the State or Government that provides superior protection against job loss and minimal demands from its workers. Exceptions noted.

The free flow of goods and capital between countries has become the enemy of "Nationalism." It was not always that way. However, with the US diminished in its industrial capacity, our country has become dependent on massive foreign purchases to sustain itself. This suggests that the United States is being maneuvered into a losing position and to become the world's first Transnational Government. Transnationalism is known by another name...One World Government. We also believe that Big Businesses and the Government share one other common imperative; both want to grow their power and control all elements that threaten that control. Think Second Amendment standing in the way. Government is like businesses and business is like the government in this very important regard. Note the overreaction to the recent Capital riots that involved no more than perhaps 500 actual individuals that entered the Capital. 450 plus or minus have been arrested according to public sources. Search for information on how many protesters entered the Capital and there are no solid estimates we could find at the time this was written. Why? Because a relatively low number of 500 people would not justify the draconian actions that followed which made Washington into an armed camp to this day.

American Government became afraid of its citizens that day. Think about that. One other observation. Media outlets were lightning quick to say "armed rebellion". No firearm was ever proved to have been brought into the capital. Likewise, the Narrative of a policeman dead by having his head bashed in with a fire extinguisher was also a falsehood. How many people know these facts?

The United States has investments (Foreign Aid, targeted business investments, and major socially driven philanthropy) in the vast majority of countries around the world. We send foreign aid to China! Not many people realize that. Did you know we partially fund the Wuhan Lab in China? Two questions follow this information. Given our largess, why does so much of the world hate us? And, why do we spend our treasure when we know it won't be successful in achieving our national goals? In too many cases, the reason is guilt over our nation's success in the past or perhaps specific narrow interests are being rewarded. How did this Groupthink begin and where is it going?

Chapter Two

Are White People Inherently Racist?

I start with a provocative question. Do White people. by virtue of their skin color, have fewer rights than any other group? We now live in a society that comes right out and says It's inappropriate to have all-white clubs, groups, and other social or business organizations. But on the other hand, it seems perfectly fine for blacks to have all-black schools, associations, and clubs. White people are constrained, not only in how they speak but also are not even allowed to teach certain subjects in schools. Cultural appropriation forbids it! Blacks can use the "N" word with impunity, but Whites will be Cancelled and excommunicated to some distant island, never to return if they reciprocate. Such words or even unproven allegations can end someone's career, resulting in extortionist demands for money, no-show fake jobs, and even more as a form of social restitution that is not that hard to see. And boy, do they love that kind of power! Let's make sure we make it clear who "they" are. Recently, a Wall Street Journal article helps to make, the question of "they" becomes abundantly clear:

Progressives Put the Racial 'Equity' Squeeze on Biden

"The left wants a spoils system on steroids. If the President gives it to them, heaven help us. President Biden...

President Biden likes to talk about "healing" and "unity," but he also keeps pledging to prioritize the supposed interests of certain favored minority groups. When is he going to realize that his goals of racial unification and racial favoritism are at cross-purposes?

Recently, President Biden signed an executive order on "racial equity." He said that George Floyd's death last summer "marked a turning point in this country's attitude toward racial justice" and is "forcing us to confront systemic racism and white supremacy." He added that "this nation and this government need to change their whole approach to the issue of racial equity" and make it "not just an issue for any single department. It has to be the business of the whole government."

Nothing quickens the pulse of progressives like talk of "systemic racism" and "white supremacy," so it's hard to know if Mr. Biden is just telling leftists what they want to hear. But if it's more than that—if the president is serious about focusing on equal outcomes instead of equal opportunities—then heaven help us. Economist Milton Friedman said the "society that puts equality before freedom will end up with neither," while "the society that puts freedom before equality will end up with a great measure of both." Of course, Friedman had a constrained view of the government's capabilities that isn't shared by very many Democrats today. For them, good intentions are what matter most.

The political left has long used racism as an all-purpose explanation for racial disparities. This philosophy ignores that disparities down through history have been the norm, not the exception and that they exist even in regions of the world where most people are of the same race. The per capita income gap between people in Eastern Europe and Western Europe, for example, is wider than the gap between whites and blacks in the U.S. Moreover, racial disparities have both grown and narrowed over time, even though racism has been constant. If Mr. Biden wants to change the government's approach to racial inequality, past history ought to inform his actions.

The greatest success of the civil-rights movement wasn't a new government program but simply getting off the backs of minorities. The "They" is the institutional collection of government officials, anti-US political groups, and a domestic and international cadre of American Haters."

The message that is communicated is that White is bad and Black is good. We wish to state the obvious, that neither is correct. But, don't say it out loud! Diners are targeted by the BLM crowds who storm into a restaurant and demand that Whites pledge allegiance to BLM and become "Antiracists." (See the example cited shortly.)

How did we cede such control over our very existence? You have heard of the so-called "Cancel Culture." Even the left is not immune from Cancel Culture. Recently the San Francisco School Board voted to strip the name from a school now named for Senator Dianne Feinstein. You dare not ask why, lest the mob of the day, led by Idealists, BLM, and the aforementioned Cancel Culture descend on you.

The **Washington Post** published the following:

"Protesters target D.C. diners, triggering backlash after heckling woman

Lauren Victor refused to go along with raising her fist — although she supports the movement "

Protesters corner diner, shout 'White silence is violence

A demonstration that began Monday evening in the District to protest the shooting of a Black man in Wisconsin wound its way through two of the city's entertainment districts, targeting diners in a tactic that has triggered a backlash online.

The crowd of protesters confronted a woman seated at a table outside a restaurant on 18th Street NW in Adams Morgan and demanded that she raise her fist in a show of solidarity.

"White silence is violence!" protesters chanted, many with fists in the air.

"Are you a Christian?" a protester demanded, yelling into her face.

But the woman, Lauren B. Victor, refused, even after her dining companion complied.

"I felt like I was under attack," Victor, 49, an urban planner and photographer who lives in the District, said in an interview afterward.

Footage of the incident went viral.

Conservatives and liberals alike agreed that the confrontational tactic was a misstep that might undermine the protest movement's intended message.

Maybe she didn't like being yelled at? Maybe she was just hungry and wanted to finish her meal? I support BLM, but I've got news for Deadspin today, I wouldn't "comply" in that situation, either. These tactics do nothing but hurt the movement. The Black Lives Matter rally, which began about 6:30 p.m. Monday at Columbia Heights Civic Plaza on 14th Street NW, drew several hundred people. In D.C., however, protesters wound their way up to 14th Street, chanting, "No Justice, No Peace," and, "Fire, fire, gentrifier — Black people used to live here."

Near Quincy Street, the crowd gathered outside restaurants, alternately accusing diners of enjoying "White privilege" and encouraging them to show support. At one table, a young man who objected to the intrusion tried to explain that he worked for a nonprofit organization committed to addressing mental health care for Black people and other underserved populations. Protesters crowded in further around the table, shining video lights in the diners' eyes and exchanging angry words.

The marchers, now about 150 strong, wound their way to Adams Morgan without further incident.

On Columbia Road, a young Black woman who was leading the protest explained the importance of engaging White people in the struggle for justice and encouraged White protesters to take the lead in confronting diners on 18th Street NW.

Several diners at other tables went along, standing or raising their fists until the crowd homed in on Victor and her companion in front of Los Cuates, a Mexican restaurant.

"I wasn't actually frightened," Victor said.

Victor said she was a supporter of the Black Lives Matter movement and had marched in previous demonstrations. But Victor said she also felt that it was wrong for hundreds of people to surround a small group of diners, approach them with their hands raised, and try to cow them into making a show of support.

"It just felt overwhelming to have all of those people come at you. To have a crowd — with all that energy — demand that you do this thing. In the moment it didn't feel right," Victor said.

"They like to think because I raise my fist it means something or other."

As the crowd moved on, Chuck Modiano continued to yell at Victor.

"Good for you — you stood your ground," Modiano said, demanding to know if she had seen the video of Blake's shooting. "We're not going to change this [expletive] for people like you."

Modiano, who identified himself as a "citizen journalist" who writes for Deadspin, said he wanted to understand her resistance.

"What was in you that you just couldn't do this?" Modiano asked. "They all did — all the other tables. You were literally the only one of 20 other people. So there was something in you that was different from all the other people."

Victor explained that she just felt coerced and somewhat threatened — although she also said she wasn't afraid.

"I didn't think anyone was actually going to do anything to me. I appreciate their anger," she said in an interview. "On one level, my best guess was no one was going to hurt me. But those things turn on a dime."

When people threaten and yell at you, I urge you...take them seriously. Dozens of people have been injured or killed by mobs in 2000. Too often mobs are getting away with violence and even murder then getting bailed out of jail by people in positions of power. Heck, we are getting away from posting bonds at all for arrests in certain liberal areas. Politicians think that it is a form of discrimination to keep someone in jail if they don't have the money to bail out. To our mind, a question of choices more than fairness. If I am frugal and have the money for bail vs. a drug user who takes every dollar they can to get high; shouldn't the distinction be fairly obvious? It sure is to most people. Crazy people are running the asylum. Ultra-liberal far-left policies are making it possible for mobs to behave lawlessly and with impunity

About 197 million non-Hispanic whites live in the U.S. today. I dare say that most white people would not believe that they foment a racist society. But you can be sure, that the Social Justice Warriors are looking for any slight, any look, whiff of superiority, anything that justifies an attack on you, the unenlightened always know more than you do.

We believe there are three different definitions of racism. They are:

- The belief that race accounts for differences in human character or ability and that a particular race is superior to others.
- Discrimination or prejudice based on race.
- The belief that each race has distinct and intrinsic attributes.

Racism is not a structural part of American idealism. Quite the contrary; freedom is the nexus requirement and is the superstructure that allows all people to excel, subject to their abilities and their propensity to strive, not race. Our central thesis on race is that in any set of individuals, from a hundred to hundreds of millions there are many people in the middle and groups on either end of the spectrum. No one can change that reality. It is a simple fact of life. That some groups excel and other lag is also a fact of life. It's biology, not politics at work. It's also a fact that Whites and the Judeo/Christian ethos built the vast majority of infrastructure, created our social mores, government, and the very economic system that made everything possible. Better to work within it, instead of attempting to dismantle it. For what reason? Your notion of what's better, fairer, or more humane? Try proving it first if you please before you destroy the best system ever created.

Capitalism or the police never were and are not an actual danger to people of color. More often than not, Capitalism has benefitted black people and the police protect black people from other blacks who do commit far more crime than their percentage of the population would be expected. Blacks in America are at the pinnacle of wealth and success as compared to Blacks in almost any other country.

The most recent FBI crime statistics available reflect the following numbers for 2018:
If we take a look at the number of violent crimes committed by blacks, we can see they committed 153,341 of the 408,873 violent crimes reported that year, which is 37% of the violent crimes. If blacks make up 13% of the population, they should only be committing

13% of the crimes, instead, they are committing crimes at a rate almost three times as many crimes as they should be. These kinds of numbers hold true in enlightened Europe and the rest of the world as well.

Statistica.com reports that a black person has a chance of being killed by police at a rate of 30 out of every million black people per year. And, even that rate is not nearly as bad as you might believe because **USA Today** recently quoted another figure of 9 unarmed black people killed by police in all of 2019, giving lie to the notion that purports blacks are being killed by the police in an almost wholesale manner. It's simply not true and goes unchallenged by a media that takes sides and no longer reliably seeks the truth. So much information, knowledge, and reputable statistics are available and would handily refute the lies. Why is the answer by people, our leaders, and the media so blatantly false to suit a political endnote rather than the truth? The answer is simple; because we are witnessing a campaign of lies, untruths, and misinformation. We are being manipulated to support someone else's narrative of what America should be.

Capitalism is the ladder that everyone climbs to be successful. Law enforcement protects us from much of the evil that circles the campfire, just out of view. Life is not finite nor preordained. Life is agnostic. God lets us lead the life we make for ourselves among the circumstances of our existence. This is the Conservative American view that exists as foundational dogma for American success and exceptionalism. This is the central thesis on which we build everything that follows.

The vast majority of Americans are not racist and they are sympathetic to the downtrodden. However, this requires effort and a positive attitude from everyone. America is the most giving nation on earth. We may believe there are differences in potential between individual Asians, Whites, Hispanics, and Blacks, but that does not alter our belief and desire for a guaranteed right to an equal start for all. It's the right thing to do.

Still, there is no embedded guarantee of success. Luck, skill, desire, and sweat, in the aggregate largely determine success or failure for each of us.

<u>Let's mention this at least one more time since it is so important. No one can guarantee an end result</u>. You can almost hear the anger of the disagreers, who yell "You can't get an equal start if we don't all have the same starting advantages." There is some truth in that. What must be kept in mind is that the choices we make or don't make when we are young inevitably affect our outcomes later in life. That we make bad choices or come from dysfunctional homes is the additive effect of generations of bad decisions and a push by multiple groups and government agencies (spreading a false narrative of untruths) which has destroyed countless lives. Such anger may be justified and is overwhelming at times, but is directed at the wrong bad actors. As we mentioned previously, life is not fair, it is agnostic. It cares not for anyone to the good or the bad.

The majority of immigrants came to this country with little more than the shirt on their backs. Yet most, and that bears repeating, most created wealth and at least a modicum of success for themselves and their families i.e. the American experience writ large. The other side, the Dark side, sees unfairness as the only essential truth of America. How else they say to explain the differences between those that have and those that do not create wealth? This type of thinking is particularly exploitable with the young, minorities, and others that have not had to strive to survive as have so few young and privileged native-born Americans. We have arrived at the point when we have a stratum of various minorities; where not all will thrive, but many still will, with or without the benefit of being white.

What the heck happened to America? Nothing focuses your attention on what is important as an empty belly. Contrary to popular belief, food resources in America are both abundant and everywhere. The effort to tap into easily obtained resources is sometimes absent. Whose fault is that? An incorrect focus on what's wrong with America paralyzes those with a propensity to believe the worst. After all, that's what they have been taught.

Chapter Three

Blind Rage and Misdirection:

But we are still getting ahead of ourselves. Imagine that America today resembles a society where a whirlwind developed and virtually every stricture and element of society are being ripped out and examined in the context of white privilege, one by one, to see if it fits an entirely new way of looking at our culture. And, exactly what is that new standard? A system of litmus tests that only reject the evils of white people, their history of slavery, economic repression, social repression, criminal justice repression, psychological oppression educational repression, human rights oppression, imperialism, medical repression, arts repression, even something called cultural appropriation. And so on and so on. We feel at times as if we, as individuals are on trial for our very beliefs, lives, and even our continued existence. Is that totally out of the question with social justice adherents swinging the ax at anything they don't like?

What we see on our television screens every day is a manifestation of how our focus has been grabbed so that we may not truly see what is more important and insidious. What could that be you say? What if the frightening events we see on TV, that present to us the wholesale destruction of the American experiment, were just the eye candy designed to keep you riveted to a single issue, a drumbeat echoing in your ears even after you stop listening or viewing? They want you to completely miss what's really going on; constant and deliberate misdirection. An attempt to rewrite history and nullify the exceptional American good done throughout the world is now what is being presented to you as Newtruth. Eventually, left unchecked, such forces expect to decapitate our social systems and wealth. That is their Endgame.

You ask: Are there actually conspiracies of people, nations, and/or groups (think the media) that have that much power, are omnipresent, staying on task decade after decade that examine us in minute detail constantly looking for any weakness to exploit? We think there are. They search for our fracture lines and stand so opposed to our way of living that, given the power, who knows what they would do? Nothing is beyond them. We believe and postulate that their views and actions are evil in the extreme.

Our enemies exist and have defined the battlefield on which we now find ourselves fighting a made-up race war theme with white nationalists counted in small numbers relevant to the size of our great land. The Destroyers dictate the terms of the fight, even as we fight for our existence playing defense on our home ground. We ceded the high ground a long time ago by being blind or failing to realize what was happening to us. If you need evidence to believe they keep trying different ways to obtain their objectives, just look backward at previous attempts by Dark forces that failed:

- 'Ban the Bomb' groups pushing for unilateral disarmament
- Violent anti-war groups were clearly provocateurs instead of what they purport to be
- Media that reports stories (or don't report them at all) in a tainted manner to favor and foster an anti-American or otherwise negative view of people and events
- 'Occupy Wall Street' was one of the first sustained efforts to highlight real but natural economic disparity, calling it evil
- Antifa is among the first modern anti-capitalism groups to advocate violence and the overthrow of our entire economic and social system
- Global Warming has become a movement used as a wedge against the United States in particular, while not so much against the rest of the world.

Climate change is being used as an excuse to reorder logical American priorities

- Critical Race Theory has become the number one excuse as to why America is evil

- Immigration has become a tool of the Destroyers to simply outnumber the producers and overwhelm the support system of the US. Read about their strategy, the **Alinsky Method** for details on this well-laid-out, and easily accessible plan to destroy America.

- The opposite of what a good education should be is controlling what is taught to young, impressionable minds. In that way, shock troops can be created for their specific cause(s). Young people today seem only able to regurgitate slogans and themes but can't think critically. At rallies, they frequently don't know why they are even there or the issues they are chanting about.

- Death of the two-parent home through government policies promotes single-parent constructs through economic rewards and a lack of stigma for children born out of wedlock.

- The even crazier, confusing, and ultimately society-splitting issue of gender identity has suddenly achieved such publicity and stature creating another wedge issue that gives one pause to question how this exploded on the scene. This is yet another example of the Emperor- has no-clothes. Redefining the very question of who is a man and who is a woman would have seemed so ridiculous just a few short years ago but the questioning of this issue is now taboo and immune even to cursory introspection.

- Valuing the least of us over the most promising of us is also a major imperative visible to all through implemented government policy which seeks to devalue hard work. Why strive at all when all outcomes should be equal?

- Being taught the greatest lie of all, that nothing is your fault and that simply trying is sufficient to keep getting your ticket punched and is the new definition of success.

- The big lie repeated over and over again by the government and special interest groups that attach no failure to our individual actions and buttress the silly notion that we need the government to keep us alive and to prevent unfairness. Big government is the problem in so many cases and that attaches to both Democrats and Republican lawmakers alike.

You can write multiple books on every point because lies and corruption are so pervasive, they have become our new normal. Collectively, all of these bullets, used individually and collectively, have thus far failed to bring down America. She stands unsteadily under the weight of all of these untruths but stands nonetheless.

But, for how long?

Chapter Four

America's Enemies:

America's enemies are not invisible but may be hard to spot at first glance. Our enemies are foreign and domestic, individuals and state actors. Who are these enemies and why would they like to see our system crumble? Some have fought us in the past and been vanquished by us either economically or on the battlefield. Many of them have very long memories of past encounters and have a desire to "settle scores." Some of our enemies see our very size, strength, and influence as unacceptable. We are a roadblock to their aspirations, or, we are an abomination to their world view in others. Our list is a veritable cornucopia of evil, deceit, and at its heart, attempted revenge against us and all we stand for. Among those that want to see us brought to heel and have the patience and wherewithal to run a long-term overarching operation like this are:

- Russia
- China
- Certain Muslim Theocracies
- World Communism/Socialism
- The One Worlders
- Super Wealthy Private Individuals or small groups of World Financiers

We do not know which of the above players is/are working in concert. However, all of the above in one way or another hate/fear the United States and would like to see our position in the world greatly diminished or even eliminated. Their individual actions prove it. In a different section of this essay, we will go into the motivations, means, and proclivities of each of these groups. What they hold in common is that they understand that the U.S. is a rich prize, believe we are weak and getting weaker, and ultimately ripe for the plucking. We represent markets, resources, future citizens of their closely held vision of the world, and more. Here is further elucidation about just a few of those "Bad Actors."

- Russia and China as state actors steal our secrets, undermine our businesses, try to foment internal discord, and attack our institutions such as higher education and our electronic infrastructure.

- A single individual, George Soros has often repeated his desire to "push the world in a cosmopolitan direction in which racism, income inequality, American empire, and the alienations of contemporary capitalism would be things of the past." This statement is quoted from a recent Guardian Article on Soros. This is Marxist rhetoric right out of the book.

- Iran is the most dangerous of the "wild cards." The very word Islam translates into "Submission." Few of our enemy's act against their own self-interest as often as Iran does. Iran and North Korea are definite exceptions. Iran is considered to be a religiously fanatical country. Ask yourself this question. How much of a jump is it from strapping a bomb on yourself and detonating it in a crowded building vs. the firing of a nuclear-tipped missile at your greatest enemy in an attempt, at a single stroke, to wipe them off the face of the Earth? Would you do that even knowing that your own country could be wiped out in the aftermath? The Mullah's of Iran sees no distinction between the two. The attainment of Paradise is what's central to their thinking and is even demanded by their religion. The theocracy of Islam knows no bounds for the destruction of infidels. And, there are plenty of true believers like those in Iran and throughout the Middle East.

Iran calls Israel the "Little Satan." Guess who the "Big Satan" is? Us. If Iran gets nuclear weapons, they know with certainty that Israel will see that as an existential threat and attack. Saudi Arabia believes the same thing about Iran. Sunnis and Shiites have been slitting each other's throats for thousands of years. Nuclear war is a near certainty if Iran or any other religious zealot obtains (develops) Nuclear weapons. Iran is feverishly working both on a nuclear device and the means to deliver it. It's not a matter of "if;", it's only a question of "when." Their rockets can already hit the U.S. mainland.

Chapter Five

How it all Began:

The vilification of America is a product of several geopolitical events over the last 100 years. Wealth coming to the Middle East in the form of oil. The failure of communism and other socialistic constructs and the incredible wealth created by the United States and all the trappings that go with it. Wealth is a form of gravity. If you have wealth, your worldview is different than if you don't have it. Particularly the children of the wealthy frequently don't understand how hard it was to achieve the wealth they were born into. You see it all the time, children who are ashamed of their affluence because it was given to them or perhaps, they are taught that it is sinful to access wealth they did not create while there are so many "problems" in the world. They want all of us to be altruistic and kind. If only it were so easy. What is wealthy is an interesting question. Many people in Middle-Class America are considered very wealthy by most of the rest of the world even if they don't feel that way themselves.

Let's get back to what has changed in America. Ever evolving, it's hard to pinpoint at what point the other side made its first moves. History has a way of not being set in stone until at least 30 years have passed, sometimes more. Our leaders and the public probably missed a lot of those first moves, because some were spectacular failures while others were never publicly or widely known. For us, we believe that our enemies targeted our education system early and often. Intellectuals, almost by definition, thrive close to educational establishments. Educators, for seemingly foolish reasons, love socialist systems that seem so much fairer, even more so after they've got themselves at the top of the food chain, gleaning the benefits of a rigged system. Teachers Unions are de facto socialist organizations that have their roots in Soviet-style communism. Don't think I'm correct? Try messing with some of the vilest, incompetent, and corrupted individuals on earth and see what happens. The vehemence of their response will be immediate, without mercy, and unkind. Wonder why children are not back in school? Ask a Teachers Union.

I don't believe Ms. Fowler would belong to a teacher's union today. Look at Chicago, New York, and LA among hundreds of liberal enclaves refusing to go back to teaching while still drawing full pay and benefits for the last year. Teachers are making it apparent who is in charge. We must stand up to the stranglehold they have on our children.

In 1966, I took my last Arithmetic class and was welcomed into the theory of New Math. The big difference was no more long-form memorization and working problems out in a static manner. Instead, theory became as important, or more important than actually being able to do (understand) math.

AmericanHeritage.com had this to say on the subject: "Before the results could even be measured, new math became a near religion, complete with its own high priests and heresies. Chief among the hierophants were the University of Illinois's Max Beberman and Stanford's Edward Begle. Together with mathematicians and educators at universities in New York, Indiana, Massachusetts, Minnesota, and Maryland, they took aim at the mindless rigidity of traditional mathematics. They argued that math could be exciting if it showed children the ways of solving rather than just the how's. Memorization and rote were wrong. Discovery, deduction, and limited drill were the best routes to arithmetical mastery."

Parents were warier back then, but we trusted our educators and the educational system that had served us so well. Ms. Fowler was my fifth-grade teacher that I introduced a moment ago and for $2400 a year, you could find no one more dedicated to her students. She was the epitome of the best kind of American teacher.

Legions of well-educated and well-adjusted children passed through her public-school door and became workers, executives, soldiers, business leaders, and yes, future teachers. Such teachers represented the best of what America was educationally. We were well taught. America flourished. But, no more.

New Math? Not so much. Were the people who pushed new Math and now Common Core seeking to codify low minimum standards to meet? No need to strive, just meet the lowest bar possible for the greatest number of children. We believe the answer to the question is fundamentally about change; changing the very idea of what is critical thinking, and undermining traditional societal norms in the process Norms which have been embraced for all time, except for the last few years. Changes that do nothing more than increase the dependency and anxiety young people feel about their future and place in society. Increased child suicides, body shaming, growing up too fast. The alternatives offered simply help the Collective continually make strides in dumbing us down, thus enabling and enhancing a massive loss of critical thinking in our country. God, there are a lot of dumb and uneducated young people. Don't you see it too? How did that happen? Acceptance of low standards, ineffective school boards, ambivalent parents, Teacher Unions, and federal involvement in the educational process are all clearly to blame. Have you seen the meager educational attainment that many school board members possess themselves? Some can't speak English! How do we expect them to raise standards? Who elects/hires such people?

Why don't parents demand better outcomes for their children? Years ago, I was speaking to a teacher where I live who had a parent complain about the summer reading list. She stated that the parents thought the list was "uppity" and made parents look bad. She finished up by stating "Are you trying to make my child smarter than me?" "Yes." And, so it goes. What would you say? Children having children. Not a great idea.

In another school, in another year, I was placed in the Advanced class for my grade. There were Basic and Intermediate classes as well. It was not too many years later that school systems had to end the practice of spending more resources on the best students and the trend began to reverse itself with spending more - or seemingly allocating equal time and money on all students. By putting children together (Mainstreaming), a system was created in which the slowest child would effectively set the pace for everyone. Predictably, discipline in school declined and children could not be easily removed from class for misbehaviors. Test scores, including SAT scores, began to decline. Endnote.org has stated or estimated that the amount spent on the approximate 10 million special needs students in our country is about double what is spent on non-special needs students. This figure is about 14% of costs for the entire student population. We question how effective special education is and what it does or does not do for the rest of the student population. Who measures these outcomes? Does anybody really know? Do they care to find out? A substantial drag on our society is all the special interest groups that have developed incredible power in how we spend public money and the policies used; frequently terrible policies with no introspection ever undertaken that do nothing to help society but are richly endowed for the benefit of few but that has a very costly and continuing overhead attached.

Like cancer, what happened in lower education moved onto the colleges and universities of America. Education became like an exclusive club for the intelligentsia, where liberal views of everything allows for a special kind of mental superiority which inevitably develops when you don't produce anything, work less, make more money than the general population and there's too little push back telling you that you don't have any clothes on with your utopian or radical ideas. You come to believe that you are enlightened when you really aren't because you are self-identified or just claim the title of Enlightened. What's always true though, is your voracious appetite for OPM (Other Peoples' Money) that is a necessary prerequisite for your individual success. You consume and produce nothing but mush minds for a living and spend money that Mother and Fathers don't have so little Johnny can get the "best" education possible. Unfortunately, Mom and Dad did not realize you were creating little Marxists, Snowflakes, Anarchists, and Antifa. After these children graduate, they either want to continue to protest unfairness, get a postgraduate degree, come home to stay a year or two and wind up hating you so much that you no longer have a relationship with your beautiful little girl. Hear the repeated demand, "Just don't forget to send me my money each month Daddy!"

The United States spends more per child than any other country in the world on education and has frighteningly low graduation rates and very low participation rates in advanced STEM degrees. Why does anyone accept these outcomes? These children are our future! Places of public education today breed mediocrity at best and create individuals unprepared to take their place in a highly competitive world economy. Public colleges and Universities learned that letting students borrow outrageous and ever-rising amounts of money for inflated educations, which graduates and non-graduates alike can't possibly pay back, was somehow a good idea. But it allowed schools to continue to build Ivory Tower buildings and pay salaries and benefits that they simply don't deserve and are not obtainable in the general economy. They are thieves of national wealth and the children entrusted to them.

Two-Thirds of post-graduate STEM spots are held by foreign students (who pay full price in general) and wicked smart domestic Asians. Why? American educators control the process and have failed the country. And it is by design. Every student that either fails and drops out or graduates but can't get the job they want/need is another soldier in the new Anti-American Army, some educators hope. It's that bad. Not every educator fits this description. But too many schools and teacher unions are strident supporters of this New America orthodoxy.

Chapter Six

30,000 Foot View:

There are three Themes to understand to explain what's happening and what is essential to keep in mind for comprehension and to translate the mainstream news when hearing it. Consider this our Rosetta Stone. These three seemingly unrelated themes are both interrelated and at the same time unrelated depending on your perspective. In some ways, you might describe these themes as threads:

- Theme A: An intensively pushed narrative that the U.S. is entering a period of extreme racial conflict. We believe that narrative to be engineered to force white retreat. But, in actuality, runs an even greater risk of evolving into a civil war. Various groups are attempting to force white people into acknowledging their past sins and transgressions, make reparations and step aside for a new generation of socially conscious "Woke" individuals who are to put our society back together in a race-aware manner. Think South African Truth and Reconciliation Trials.

Have you heard of Identity politics? This is a political philosophy in which groups of people having a particular racial, religious, ethnic, social, or cultural identity tend to promote their specific interests or concerns without regard to the interests or concerns of any larger political group as the driving force. This is the subtext or <u>Base Thread</u> oh-so-popular today.

- Theme B: That the idea behind Theme A is nothing more than a Strategy of the Destroyers to weaken the United States' influence, industrial production, and to encourage an influx of low-skill migrants. Further, to reduce the concept of

American individualism, eliminate our belief in historic American exceptionalism, and willingly give up essential freedoms given to us by our Creators and enshrined in our Constitution. This is the Operational objective and we call it the <u>Worker Thread</u>.

- Theme C: The Endgame is effective absorption of the United States into some kind of world Collective run by interests known and unknown whose role is to provide the Collective and its leaders with material resources, labor, and political backing for their ends. This is a Strategic Strategy honed and refined over a lengthy period of time. The <u>Endgame Thread</u>. Our enemies have their own dilemmas. They want to destroy us a political, social, and economic system, but keep us as consumers and producers. After all, at the top of the heap will be whatever new politburo is created and the top will need their special products, services, and especially luxuries their hard work deserves.

Chapter Seven

Why This Essay?

No one can hope to win a war without understanding these three things:

1. Knowing and acknowledging we are in fact, at war
2. Learning who is the real enemy(s)?
3. Determining a successful strategy to win the war

It was easy to know we were at war when Japan attacked us on December 7th, 1941. The enemy was understood, the choices we had before us were clear, and although a pacifist nation just 24 hours before, in an instant we became a nation out for vengeful blood. We never questioned ourselves again as to the virtue of our fight. Whatever the sacrifice, whatever the privation, collectively we were all in. That's how you fight and win wars.

For our friends that believe that big things, like attitudes to fighting a war, can't change overnight. Keep in mind that a week before Pearl Harbor two-thirds of American adults thought the United should sit out the next war in Europe. The day after Pearl Harbor, that number reversed itself. We are relying on that kind of change of heart once the population understands that they have been duped by their leaders and War came to us without the population being told.

We knew we were at war when on September 11th, 2001 when we were attacked, but with who and why? Politicians took more than a few days to tell the American people exactly what was going on and what we were going to do about it. In fact, that became a moving and ever-expanding process that was not fully formed for two full years. The only name anyone heard about was Osama Bin Laden. And, it took us more than ten years to get him. Messaging matters and not nearly as many Americans were on board with the fight on Terrorism as were against the Japanese. Universal buy-in was never achieved and as a result, we were not all in. Our ability to fight was constrained by a body politic unable or unwilling to go "all in." Wars are only won when you are prepared to go "all in." Any other war will fail on multiple levels. War can be defined simply as "Killing people and breaking things." Any other objective is not war but rather a form of policing or an insurgency. It is important to know when you have crossed the Rubicon and are actually at war. It must not be an accident, but a cold calculating conclusion to engage the enemy and destroy him. Citizens must achieve buy-in whenever we decide to go to war. And, having made that awesome commitment, be prepared to outlast, outgun and be just as brutal as your enemy as we determined necessary at Hiroshima and Nagasaki. When you meet the objectives that took you to war in the first place, declare victory and go home. Every war needs a predetermined exit ramp.

The United States has been under attack for more than a generation. The closest analogy we can think of is a comparison to the Cold War. While a World War III fight with the Soviets was possible, all parties realized there would be no winners, only losers. A new kind of war was needed. One that could be decisively won. That new kind of war is called "Unrestricted War," thought of and implemented by none other than the Chinese. In 1999. **Gregory R. Copley**, a Historian, Author, and Strategic Analyst wrote:

"Beijing made it clear in 1999 that when it went to war with the US it would be a new kind of war.

People's Republic of China (PRC) Pres. Xi Jinping then announced in October 2018 that he had begun a "new 30 Years War" with the US.

But there was no "Pearl Harbor" moment, so the rest of the world disregarded the declaration of war. That was a mistake.

It became clear that the 2020 COVID-19-inspired "global fear pandemic" laid out the battlefield terrain and saw the opening shots emerge from the PRC in a variety of strategic formats. To be sure, COVID-19 was not itself the "Pearl Harbor moment"; it was the subsequent *fear pandemic* that drove down the global economy.

Beijing could not wait any longer to begin strategic operations — the new form of "total war" — if it was to survive as a global power and to assume primacy within its symbolic 30-year time frame.

Keep in mind that China is only one of several "suspects." Acting alone or in concert with other nations, the Chinese are major threats to our nation regardless. It's hard to believe that such a disparate group of anti-US groups is working together, but on some level, they are aligned and in sync with each other.

There are literally thousands of "Think Tanks" worldwide. Just imagine for a moment that America's enemies had their own "How to Destroy America" Think Tank. They probably do. What would be the most effective policy measures and actions you could devise to weaken American influence and what would effectively work to chip away at its social, political, and economic underpinnings in the most effective, yet stealthy manner? Finally, how would you bring the country to its knees in order to inject/substitute a different system more aligned with its aims and aspirations?

Ever gone on a car trip with the kids saying over and over "Are we there yet?" Cute, the first three or four times, annoying the next 2 or three times, and exceptionally irritating thereafter. And, so it is with our enemies. Americans who care about world politics are few and far between. We break down like this. 50% of people are totally self-absorbed and only if their cell phone did not work or Facebook became unavailable would they even look up and have an interest in what's going on. This group is what we will call the Animal Farm class. The best they can do is parrot some phrases like "White Bad, Diversity Good."

25% of people knowing something bad is going on around them, but still, feel powerless to affect anything much greater than their next meal. They worry about the future only occasionally because it gives them a headache and too deeply involved with routines they seek to perpetuate in their daily lives. This class of people is only marginally more aware than the Animal Farm class but are possibly persuadable.

15% of people have strong feelings about a variety of issues but never question how each issue interrelates to other issues. They are easily influenced by "feelings" rather than logic, because, hey! Logic is tough!

Now, we are left with the classic 10% of the people, the 90-10 rule you always hear about. This 10% includes both our internal and external enemies and the smaller body of citizens, both aware and unaware, or motivated, or not so much...yet. The two sides on the field are analogous to a pro sports team vs. little leaguers. That pro sports team working actively to defeat the United States is very organized and has been at this for a long time. Our little league Patriots have a lot of spirit and bluster but are unorganized, unfocused, inadequately led, and at best, are full of future potential, not yet realized. They need time to season and mature. And they will. Until then, at the very pinnacle of our Patriots are an elite group of Command, Control, Communications, and Intelligence assets being organized, formed, and being readied, should it come to that. How do we know they exist? Nature abhors a void. There are too many people thinking about what's coming without a nucleus of Patriots already working the problem. Trust me on that!

The difference between our side and theirs? One has a central "Think Tank" keeping it focused on the right direction for them, while the Patriots are still largely lost in understanding and committing to their future role. We must admit that great thinkers and leaders on our side exist, but they are "Sub Rosa" for now.

This brings us to our first conclusion of this chapter. If you are a Patriot, you must understand the problem and know that you missed the start of the war. You weren't invited, but the other side did get their invitation and accepted! Patriots, almost by definition are the good guys (and girls) that simply have not spun up... yet. But the enemy is not only coming, they are already here. At the time this was written there is a paranoid view in Washington which has thousands of soldiers protecting not you, but instead, the Washington Elite, those that see themselves as somehow better than the average citizen. What are they afraid of? Time to talk some more about our enemies.

Chapter Eight

China:

"The PRC will not hesitate to use force to defeat and reverse any attempt at containing the historic ascent of China to becoming the global Hegemon comes 2049." Attributed to **Xi Jinping** formally instructing the PLA to start preparing for war with the United States.

Why don't we take people at their word? **Hitler** told us what he was going to do. **Mao** did as well. This is not hyperbole. This is the truth that seems way over the head of most Americans, including its politicians to conceive and accept. And two, it galvanizes our enemy for the mission ahead. Sacrifice is a word Americans have forgotten. However, it is a daily mantra for our enemies who are astounded at how easy it has been to manipulate American society.

China considers us an enemy. They tell us so. However, they also need us to buy their goods. In 2019, China-Mike.com reported that 18% of all Chinese manufacturing is exported to the United States. Also, another 5-10% of Chinese output goes to third-party countries but is ordered by US companies. That 23% to 28% is like a dagger to the throat of China. This is a threat to China's voracious need for more industrial work. President Donald Trump was China's worst nightmare. Virtually every President before him recognized the "China Problem" but was unwilling to deal with it. Trump's Tariff Policy, far from being the failure that was predicted, restrained China on several fronts. China's actions in the South China Sea, building heavily defended and fortified dredged islands in disputed territory claimed by no less than nine other nations, have pulled together in opposition, including:

- NATO and SEATO nations

- US
- Australia
- Viet Nam
- India
- Philippines
- New Zealand
- Malaysia
- Taiwan
- Singapore

And more every month or so.

China seeks to isolate the United States all over the world with a strategy entitled "The Belt and Road Initiative." The **Belt and Road Initiative (BRI**, or **B&R)**, known in Chinese and formerly in English as **One Belt One Road** or **OBOR. It** is a global infrastructure development strategy adopted by the Chinese government in 2013 to invest and interfere in nearly 70 countries and international organizations. How many American's know that the Panama Canal is now run by China under a management contract with Panama? Do they even care? They should.

An example of how dangerous and bold China is: America's latest nuclear weapon design was stolen as discussed in the following 1999 **CNN** article:

"WASHINGTON (CNN) -- China has been stealing America's most sensitive nuclear secrets "for at least the past several decades" and despite high-level knowledge of the thefts, security at U.S. nuclear labs still "does not meet even minimal standards," according to a congressional report recently released.

Beijing could begin testing the first of its advanced nuclear weapons based on its information stolen from others as early as this year and it could be deployed as soon as 2002, according to the Cox report.

"The stolen U.S. nuclear secrets give (China) design information on thermonuclear weapons on a par with our own," the report says.

"With the stolen U.S. technology, (China) has leaped, in a handful of years, from 1950s-era strategic nuclear capabilities to the more modern thermonuclear weapons designs."

So damaging is the stolen information, the report concludes, it "could have a significant effect on the regional balance of power, particularly concerning Taiwan."

Chapter Nine

China is not our friend:

What other evil mischief are they capable of? Cyber Warfare anyone? Shooting down our satellites in orbit? Currency manipulation? Rare Earth mineral monopoly? Work with our enemies against us? Support North Korea in defiance of international law? Will China continue to steal every bit of Intellectual Property it can? Counterfeit US Currency? Assassinate Chinese citizens on US soil? Chances are that if you can name it, they've done it or will do it soon.

An important point that very few in the US are aware of is that there are no legal niceties about who is in charge in China. Here, we have people, companies, State and Local governments, laws, statutes, and more, all can say they are "in charge." In China, the Communist Party and the State are one. The State "allows" limited personal and corporate rights and frequently owns or controls its important companies. No one does anything in China against the State or they might find their families receiving a "bill" from the State charging them for the bullet used to execute their loved one. I kid you not. Amnesty International states China executes more people each year than all other nations combined.

The concept of "Face" is incredibly important to Asians in general and China in particular. Ritual and custom are built into every level of Chinese discourse. China expects foreigners to play the game too. As far as we can tell, China has been successful at making American Foreign Policy dance to their tune ever since Nixon opened China with Kissinger way back in 1971. President Trump upset that apple cart with charges of currency manipulation, assessing tariffs on Chinese goods, and pursuing charges of Unfair Trade Practices. Think Hong Kong. Did you know that China is largely exempt from significant change under the Paris Climate Agreement?

China enjoys "Most Favored Nation Status" in dealings with us. Effectively, this means we treat them as if they are a developing country and give them many economic benefits that we don't give to our other "developed trading partners. It can be argued that the United States built modern China from scratch and imbued it with every technological advantage we have and then opened markets for them to sell too often at the loss of opportunities for our country, people, and companies. Given that the 1.2-billion-person market dwarfs ours; have we taught ourselves to be loyal to a new master...China? Think we are overstating the importance of China to U.S. companies?

ChinaDaily.com wrote: "The overwhelming majority of US companies are making profits and witnessing unprecedented progress in intellectual property protection in China, yet they also felt the pinch of the trade tensions between the world's two biggest economies."

The annual member survey, completed in June on 100 major US companies — about half of the USCBC membership, found 97 percent of the companies responded "yes" to the question "Are your China operations profitable?"

"The vast majority of companies report their China operations are profitable – so much so that the number of respondents reporting a profit margin rate for their China operations that is higher than that of their overall operations jumped from 38 percent to 46 percent in 2019," it said. And, "The overwhelming majority of US companies are making profits and witnessing unprecedented progress in intellectual property protection in China, yet they also felt the pinch of the trade tensions between the world's two biggest economies," according to a survey released by the US-China Business Council on Thursday.

So here is your takeaway. US Corporations act in the same manner as individuals do so for reasons of greed and self-interest. Keep in mind, they are in fact, not individuals and no one should think otherwise. They will do what is good for them at the expense of what is best for their home country unless precluded otherwise. Corporations enjoy unique benefits that require them to be good citizens. The question is, of their home country, or the world? We want our corporations to be Nationalistic and to support the US. A policy of "America First", just like China and many other nations.

Corporations are ultimately two things:

a. Corporations are an important part of a nation's economic productivity and should be considered a strategic national resource.

b. Corporations are run by men (and women) who are corruptible. China has myriad ways of corrupting these individuals.

In the end, China allows foreigners in their country for three purposes:

a. For access to foreign capital that was not previously accessible

b. For the intellectual property, foreigners can bring to the table

c. To create jobs in China so that China can be in a better position both economically and militarily. Many technologies are dual-use, i.e., a helicopter can be used for Search and Rescue or to launch missiles or deliver troops.

When China is eventually done with us and thousands of American companies in China have received their orders to divest or return home, will they think it was a good ride, but time to go home? Or will Americans feel betrayed as the next arrow in China's quiver is pulled out and launched to a seemingly unsuspecting and hapless enemy that never saw it coming? Just think about the effect on major industrials like **GE, Caterpillar, Chevron, Boeing,** and hundreds of other companies when they lose a significant slice of their world markets in an instant. Where's our protection against that? Remember, The **Chinese Communist Party** has no legal strictures that preclude them from doing just that when the time is right and when the war escalates and becomes overt instead of covert. Our seed corn companies, the beating heart of our economy will find themselves in competition with China on the world stage with a competitor who has a much lower cost structure, equal technology (that they stole from us) and has therefore become more competitive than us. That is the ultimate result of an appeasement policy.

The US will come to rely on its home markets and perhaps those of certain trading partners in similar straits as ourselves. Not a good position to be in, but perhaps better than losing our national sovereignty, our technology, and our military edge. The degree of greediness we wind up with will either stabilize us or see us fall down the rabbit hole of collaboration with the enemy. Will we be ready for tough choices? It has not recently been in our nature to do hard things. Hardened and tough we must be. When you face intractable enemies, you too must engage them on their level.

China is demonstrably in opposition to the United States on virtually every subject. Even when they are not in actual opposition to our aims and goals, they will still take a public position in opposition to us anytime they can, simply to weaken our position. We see these examples in myriad issues:

- North Korea proliferating nuclear weapons with China's acquiescence
- Stable economic markets are elusive as China manipulates them for their benefit
- Iran and missile proliferation technology also supported by China
- Iran and Nuclear technology supported by China
- China positions itself in Africa as a non-GMO seed substitute to U.S. offerings even as our yields are greater and we largely give the seed away anyway.
- Fishing yield disputes and loss of territorial access leading to reduced catches for the rest of the world
- Attempting to keep markets to themselves through intimidation and threats. A good example is Japan has been warned by China that Africa is a "home market" of China.

- Buying the only major rare earth mineral producer in the United States and then shutting it down so they have greater control over the world market.

And, there are many more examples.

Somewhere in this treatise, we feel compelled to discuss in a little more detail Covid-19 and China's role in potentially spreading the virus throughout the world. Did you know that China is the only country on earth that grew economically in 2020? According to the UK's "The Express" China has officially reported a total of 3,342 deaths from Covid. In a country of 1.2 billion, how is that strikingly low number possible? The only way that seems reasonable was if they were prepared for the virus with foreknowledge. And, with that knowledge and the power that only a dictatorship possesses, they did the quarantining necessary to stop the virus in its tracks.

But, China did let it out of the country to run amuck among all other countries of the world. Remember, it was China who was ready, willing, and able, to sell us anything we needed, like PPE for which they seemed to have an overabundance, as well as pharmaceuticals and other durable goods for a price. No altruism here. China profited off of the world pandemic.

Coincidence? Maybe. But shouldn't we all be a little more circumspect? Ask yourself this question; would you put it past them? In our opinion; this was an act of calculated biological warfare in retaliation for the economic fight we were clearly winning before March 2021. And, they've gotten away with it. "Nothing to see, move along folks" is what our government now says. Recently, WHO, which we immediately rejoined after President Biden took office, made a statement to the effect that it was "Highly Unlikely" that the virus came from the Wuhan labs although on-site inspections were badly limited. That is an exercise in raw power by China, over WHO, and member countries. Did you know that we just signed a new three-year contract funding the Wuhan lab? What's that all about? We want answers.

Chapter Ten

Other Bad Actors plus Attacks on Capitalism and Individualism:

We mentioned both State Actors such as Iran and North Korea, but there are two other classes of enemies. Those are our traditional philosophical enemies and the newest member of the Klan...World Dominators. It is beyond the scope of this document to go through each and every existential threat the US faces. World Dominators are a new one. Where is your proof, you ask? Ever heard of Dark Matter? While accepted by science as real, we can neither view it, measure it, weigh it or use any of our traditional means of proving its existence. We infer it scientifically. And, so it is with the diabolical World Dominators. Suspected of existing in various forms since the end of WWII, there have been powerful groups of sometimes unaligned people, companies, and institutions that don't accept the basic concept and imposition of Capitalism or the US as the de facto and lone superpower in the world. They see our system, our success as their own existential threat. An important truism we'd like to share is that the coexistence of Good and Evil in the world is inconsistent. One must triumph over the other. Inevitably, there will be a day of reckoning where one must annihilate the other. Our enemies know that, but if we choose to ignore the empirical evidence before us of the existence of Good and Evil and close our eyes to the threat, the threat remains regardless of whether or not we wish it would go away.

That American **Capitalism** has created the greatest amount of wealth and prosperity the world has ever known is not really in dispute. The empirical facts are stark. The fact that it did so quickly is not in dispute. That capitalism raises all boats is not in dispute. Those that are against Capitalism hold that belief for several reasons. Among them are:

- It's a seemingly random system. Winners and Losers are not predetermined. Rich people start companies and fail spectacularly, and poor people start companies and create brands known all over the world.

- The distribution of Goods and Services is not evenly calculated. You must pay for what you take, a concept held in low regard by many people in the world who think much of what you need to live on is to be considered as a fundamental right.

- It creates a system of outsiders, workers, managers, owners, and at the very apex, the one-percenters who are, a particularly vilified group of people who couldn't possibly deserve what they have according to those that despise them.

- The State does not run the means of productions, does not set quotas, does not restrain trade, and entry by new entrants is encouraged and more. It's a disorganized system that simply bothers many people because it is not predictable. Of course, we don't live under "Pure Capitalism" anymore, which may be one of the reasons why Capitalism is under attack.

- It's been said that Capitalism is the worst system ever created, except for all the others. Capitalism as in Free Traders almost always beat every other system, making them look bad. Wars have been started just on that fact alone.

- Israel was reviled by most of its neighbors because of Israel's unparalleled economic success, without oil as a revenue enhancer, Israel just made many Arab countries look terrible. There was a conference in 1962 in El Akaba where one of the attendees joked "Maybe we should partner with Israel under the name the United Herab Republic". He was executed shortly thereafter. This is no laughing matter to Arab leaders.

- Capitalism is never perfect. Rule number one of Capitalism is that the only right you have is the right to go broke. Capitalism is about risk and reward. Unless the government puts its thumb on the scale, inevitably there will be winners and losers. The only thing worse is when the government puts its finger on the scale. Governments rarely pick authentic winners, and their picks typically fail spectacularly.

Chapter Eleven

Can We Win? And Who is John Galt?"

Atlas Shrugged written in 1957 is my favorite book. The issues were the same then as now, 63 years later. That is nothing more than astounding. We encourage everyone to read this foundational book.

Comment's courtesy of The **Burning Platform** blog incorporated herein.

John Galt's speech in Ayn Rand's Atlas Shrugged is over 33 thousand words, but these passages capture the essence of Going Galt:

> *"For twelve years, you have been asking: Who is John Galt? This is John Galt speaking. I am the man who loves his life. I am the man who does not sacrifice his love or his values. **I am***

the man who has deprived you of victims and thus has destroyed your world, and if you wish to know why you are perishing—you who dread knowledge—I am the man who will now tell you.

You have heard it said that this is an age of moral crisis. You have said it yourself, half in fear, half in hope that the words had no meaning. You have cried that man's sins are destroying the world and you have cursed human nature for its unwillingness to practice the virtues you demanded. Since virtue, to you, consists of sacrifice, ***you have demanded more sacrifices at every successive disaster****. In the name of a return to morality, you have sacrificed all those evils which you held as the cause of your plight. You have sacrificed justice to mercy. You have sacrificed independence to unity. You have sacrificed reason to faith. You have sacrificed wealth to* *need. You have sacrificed self-esteem to self-denial. You have sacrificed happiness to duty.*

You will win when you are ready to pronounce the oath I have taken at the start of my battle— and for those who wish to know the day of my return, I shall now repeat it to the hearing of the world:

I swear—by my life and my love of it—that I will never live for the sake of another man, nor ask another man to live for mine."

The key point is to deprive the Marxist/Deep State/Oligarchy of victims who they can use to further their warped, nonsensical, totalitarian agenda of control, force, and wealth extraction for the greater good – of the oligarchs. They create a crisis with their laws, regulations, legislation, mandates, executive orders, and decrees and then make it far worse with their "solutions", while demanding more sacrifices by the little people to keep their sinking ship afloat. This is their Achilles heel.

If millions of individuals Go Galt and Starve the Beast, one transaction at a time, withdrawing our consent because we believe those governing us are illegitimate, the State lacks the enforcement power and means to punish people they cannot find or identify as criminals. This is guerilla warfare in a modern technological dystopian world. Each of us has different life circumstances, financial capacity, and constraints, but everyone can contribute something to toppling our oppressors. Here are some thoughts. I am sure you can creatively add to this list:

If ever an opponent had a choleric temper, it is the Marxist regime currently in power, with the hateful Pelosi, wrathful Schumer, venomous AOC, angry Biden, malevolent Harris, and malicious Deep State apparatchiks easily irritated and can be goaded into making irrational decisions. Their arrogance, lack of self-awareness, and continuous barefaced hypocrisy leave them exposed to ridicule and scorn on a daily basis, which makes them angrier and more susceptible to contempt and mockery from their opponents.

There is no need to interrupt the enemy when they continue to issue executive orders and pass legislation that will have disastrous consequences. Even though the Reddit guys eventually had their asses handed to them, they proved a strategized sneak attack by the little guys could create havoc and disarray on Wall Street. The entire episode tore back the curtain and revealed the game is perpetually rigged in favor of billionaire hedge fund managers and the Wall Street cabal.

This war is winnable if we use Irish Democracy and Going Galt tactics and out-think our narcissist, intellectually deficient, liberal arts major enemies. The danger is when they become frustrated by being out-smarted and out-maneuvered, they will lash out violently against men who just want to be left alone to live their lives as free men. When the financial system implodes, and it certainly will, they will attempt to scapegoat the deplorables.

If they endeavor to violently enforce their mandates, they will unleash hardened men who will give no quarter in inflicting their vengeance upon those who chose not to leave them to peacefully live their lives. The electrical grid and government computer systems are highly susceptible to attack. Strategic strikes of truckers could create food shortages in a matter of days in Democrat-run urban enclaves that will switch from peaceful protests to violent and deadly battlefields when empty bellies become the norm.

The 300 million guns in this country are owned by men who know how to use them. These political animals will pay a dear price for awakening the inner **Outlaw Josey Wales** in millions of angry men. This unattributed quote captures what will happen when they push us too far.

Chapter Twelve

Winning this Battle Requires Three Things:

1. Knowing who the enemy(s) is
2. Resisting and refusing to be another one of their victims
3. Everything is on the table

Are you willing to give up comfort today for the future of your children and our country? Are you willing to reject grey thinking vs. binary black and white conclusions to embrace truth and light? Or, are you willing to live life in fear and dumb as a Delta minus as in the book **Brave New World**?

If you want to resist the Darkness, you need not pick up a gun and shoot the nearest politician who you believe is an anti-American Destroyer and traitor. Instead, resistance can be non-violent and persistent. Resistance means that, at every opportunity and every juncture of life, choose to be life-affirming and do what is right for you as an individual and for your family. Help your friends and neighbors understand what's at stake and persuade them to resist. Direct them to authoritative sources of information, discuss issues, find solutions, and vote en masse. Express your personal rights, know what they are, and let no one dissuade you from using every one of those rights at every opportunity you have. Do not be cowed by fear, don't be embarrassed to be seemingly standing alone. Together we are an unstoppable force.

Yes, we can win. The fatal flaw in the planning by our enemies is that they need us to destroy ourselves. They can't do it overtly. They are depending on us to tear ourselves apart like some mindless machine that is out of balance. America is an Exceptional nation. We have millions of people, White, Black, Asian, and Hispanic that value American exceptionalism. (We have a growing Hispanic population that is enjoying the American dream more and more every day. They represent the worst nightmare for the Destroyers who need societal failure to create more dependency and not less.)

The secret of most successful rebellions is that they are typically asymmetric. Just as our enemies have used small groups of Fifth Columnists to do their bidding, we have Patriots willing to give their all to reset the clock and return America to its admittedly imperfect self. We don't need millions of people taking to the streets with guns. Standing together and saying in one breath "I am an American, I am imbued with certain unalienable rights. We stand together for the common good and will brook no interference with our individual rights. You either stand with us or against us."

Listen to this quote from the Declaration of Independence of the United States of America written in 1776:

"Prudence, indeed, will dictate that Governments long established should not be changed for light and transient causes; and accordingly, all experience hath shewn, that mankind are more disposed to suffer, while evils are sufferable, than to right themselves by abolishing the forms to which they are accustomed. But when a long train of abuses and usurpations, pursuing invariably the same Object evinces a design to reduce them under absolute Despotism, it is their right, it is their duty, to throw off such Government, and to provide new Guards for their future security."

I have a friend who always talked about Mr. Froggy. That a frog will sit in a pan of cold water and even when you turn up the heat to high, he won't jump out until it is too late. And so it is with too many people. They wait until it is too late. Don't be Mr. Froggy.

I hear some doubters among you. Things have changed but they are still recognizable, and things are not that bad, you say. A friend caught themselves from protesting as a consequence of some terrible service they received. In the past, they would have left zero tip, called a manager over, or scolded the individual. Do you also remember doing that in the past? People are much more passive now and less likely to do or say something for fear of retribution. It's happened to me and it probably happened to you. This is not a good thing; it's that little person sitting on your shoulder warning you there's danger in calling someone out. Especially if that person is a protected class, which is everyone except for white straight males. Let that sink in.

Chapter Thirteen

Why the Second Amendment is the last line of defense:

"Everything is on the Table." Historian Patrick Charles wrote:

"The Second Amendment to the Constitution of the United States, adopted in 1791 as part of the Bill of Rights, that provided a constitutional check on congressional power under Article I Section 8 to organize, arm and discipline the federal militia. The Second Amendment reads, "A well regulated Militia, being necessary to the security of a free State, the right of the people to keep and bear Arms, shall not be infringed." Referred to in modern times as an individual's right to carry and use arms for self-defense, the Second Amendment was envisioned by the Framers of the Constitution, according to College of William and Mary law professor and future U.S. District Court judge St. George Tucker in 1803 in his great work Blackstone's Commentaries: With Notes of Reference to the Constitution and Laws of the Federal Government of the United States and the Commonwealth of Virginia, as the "true palladium of liberty." In addition to checking federal power, the Second Amendment also provided state governments with what Luther Martin (1744/48–1826) described as the "last coup de grace" that would enable the states "to thwart and oppose the general government." Last, it enshrined the ancient Florentine and Roman constitutional principle of civil and military virtue by making every citizen a soldier and every soldier a citizen."

There may come a time that calls for an entirely different approach. We see the opposition taking to the streets killing our citizens and police, taking land, occupying buildings, seizing property, and burning some of those buildings to the ground. Insurance companies paid out more money for the destruction of property in riots in

2020 than any previous time. Civil authorities virtually encourage this kind of behavior with little to no Police/National Guard participation, zero bail, and politicians egging on the violence. We are listening to the message they are sending.

Citizens with loved ones to protect, homes to keep safe, and businesses they actually built Mr. Obama will fight. Do you want proof? Last year broke every record for gun and ammunition purchases. Millions and millions of previously unarmed citizens armed themselves. You can hardly buy any ammunition even today as unprecedented shortages of ammo continue. You don't have to be a mind reader to figure out that people are scared. They are scared of what they see, what they hear, and what they saw in an election that for the first time must be questioned.

All of these new and existing gun owners are tomorrow's infantry. And the government knows it and wants to do everything they can to neuter and neutralize the threat. How many of you could imagine Concertina wire encircling the capital and being defended as if a wartime objective? Mind-boggling! The government has now officially become afraid of its people. Militias, paranoids, criminals? The government was/is not afraid of them. They are afraid of you. This is unparalleled and gives all of us a head's up of sorts. And that the current administration is more than willing to take on its own people in pursuit of unpopular objectives. They know better than you do and they are willing to kill some portion of the citizenry to get their way. This is different than anything before. Let me tell you a little story that few people know about that demonstrates the lack of restraint the government can be counted on to employ. Ever heard of the "Bonus Army?"

From Wikipedia:

The Bonus Army was a group of 43,000 demonstrators – made up of 17,000 U.S. World War I veterans, together with their families and affiliated groups – who gathered in Washington, D.C. in mid-1932 to demand early cash redemption of their service certificates. Organizers called the demonstrators the "Bonus Expeditionary Force", to echo the name of World War I's American Expeditionary Forces, while the media referred to them as the "Bonus Army" or "Bonus Marchers". The demonstrators were led by Walter W. Waters, a former sergeant.

Many of the war veterans had been out of work since the beginning of the Great Depression. The World War Adjusted Compensation Act of 1924 had awarded them bonuses in the form of certificates they could not redeem until 1945. Each certificate, issued to a qualified veteran soldier, bore a face value equal to the soldier's promised payment with compound interest. The principal demand of the Bonus Army was the immediate cash payment of their certificates.

On July 28, 1932, U.S. Attorney General William D. Mitchell ordered the veterans removed from all government property. Washington police met with resistance, shot at the protestors, and two veterans were wounded and later died. President Herbert Hoover then ordered the U.S. Army to clear the marchers' campsite.

Army Chief of Staff General Douglas MacArthur commanded a contingent of infantry and cavalry, supported by six tanks. The Bonus Army marchers with their wives and children were driven out, and their shelters and belongings burned.

A second, smaller Bonus March in 1933 at the start of the Roosevelt administration was defused in May with an offer of jobs with the Civilian Conservation Corps at Fort Hunt, Virginia, which most of the group accepted. Those who chose not to work for the CCC by the May 22 deadline were given transportation home. In 1936, Congress overrode President Roosevelt's veto and paid the veterans their bonus nine years early.

Yes. Government serves its own needs above the citizen's needs they swore to protect. They are depending on you to be compliant. Many of us will not be.

Truth is not situational; it is the truth or not. One plus one must always equal two. No argument, no emotional outburst, no wanting it to be something else changes that essential truth, no matter what people tell you or any new math may have you believe! I state to you that my life is my own. No one else is responsible for it other than me. Consequently, I am not responsible for the acts of others and we will not be made to pay for the sins of our Fathers, other individuals, or the government we live under.

Chapter Fourteen

The Question of: "Can Voting Force an End of America As We Know It?

Is the right of the people to vote and change our system of values absolute? Can voters go to the polls tomorrow and vote to have a King or adopt a Communist Manifesto? Or, open our borders and invite the entire world in? Make D.C., Puerto Rico, or Guatemala for that matter a State? How about creating a Wealth Tax that says the government can confiscate everything you own above $100,000? Today, the ballot box is being used in a manner not contemplated by the Founding Fathers. We believe that the Declaration of Independence inferred one additional right not available in the Constitution. The right to "throw off such Government, and to provide new Guards for their future security." That passage from the

Declaration of Independence was the go-ahead to fight a tyrannical government in general by any means necessary. It was true when we, as a Colonial Colony demanded freedom, independence, and self-rule. It is true today where we demand much the same thing. Many would argue that our form of self-rule has become contorted. Others will point out that freedom without responsibility has created a government devoted to giving things to the people in return for future votes. I don't know how we fix that, but the ability to "vote" yourself stuff was a real concern of the Founding Fathers even back then. In the past, we have had more or less, relatively good leaders. Today...not so much. Partisan politics has its roots in the election of individuals who are frequently neither highly educated, wise nor particularly sage nor believers in Capitalism, freedom, and democracy. They are in it for the power and perks they can receive ostensibly being public servants. Why should we be surprised when they vote for selfish interests? The lack of term limits is one of the only things the Founding Fathers got wrong. However, they never contemplated that people would be elected to the Senate or House and could then become wealthy staying for an unlimited number of terms.

You must be at least 50 years old to remember how America used to be the ultimate and undisputed force for good in the world. And, that it has largely been replaced by what we have today, a shadow of our former magnificence. Contrary to the ever-popular "you can't turn back the clock." I submit that we must turn that clock back and realize that the actions of a few, subverted America, and our way of life. It would only be natural to beat that enemy and restore the intentional harm done to us all. We prize our history; we revel in the personal freedoms and liberties we once had. We cannot contemplate a nation where what is true and necessary is subsumed by the "I'm OK, you're OK mentality." We want, no we demand our nation back before it's past the point of no return as the Destroyers now intend.

Fellow Americans, I proffer to you today that we have reached that time. Indeed, it is past time for us all to get up off the floor, stand on our own two legs and no longer suffer the indignity and crushing force of despotism that so easily has pervaded our great land. "This is your country if you can keep it" attributed to Ben Franklin, has now become painfully real.

Will you keep It? I ask each and every one of you to consider your role in saving our wonderful little experiment called the United States of America before it becomes but a footnote in time. Not all of you will answer the call. But enough of us must find the intestinal fortitude to step up, just as the Minutemen of history. Minutemen were the first to fight, organizing themselves, training, observing, strategizing, and ultimately in the fight against tyranny. History has a way of repeating itself. Look to the future without dread. The future is full of opportunity and promise. As the New Minutemen (and women) the day will dawn once again when the American Flag flies proud and strong.

God Bless America

Allan J. Feifer
Bald Point, Florida

About the Author

Allan J. Feifer was born in 1956 in Atlanta, GA to Beverly and Bernard Feifer, a successful Animal Feed Manufacturer and Real Estate Developer. Allan started flying when he was just 13, had his first solo flight at 16 and became a certified instrument pilot before he was 18. From just 8 years old, Allan worked various jobs in his Father's company after school, learning to operate heavy equipment, helping design and acquire industrial equipment, and purchasing for the Company.

At 17 he left home to work with his Father's chief engineer Mario Salvador, who was doing construction work in Nicaragua at the time. Mario and Allan started a company ferrying aircraft from the United States to Latin America and eventually did contract flying for an agency of the US government. That partnership expanded in the late 70's when Mario and Allan formed a company called DEC International (DEC) to fill a new niche in "conflict construction." The company did work over the years in Latin America, the Middle East and Africa. Tragically, Mario was killed in a plane crash in

Columbia in 1981, leaving Allan as the sole owner of the company.

Starting during the first Gulf War, DEC engaged in construction work for Ariel Sharon, who was Israel's Minister of Housing at the time and later became Prime Minister of Israel. During that time, Allan also met Deputy Housing Minister Benjamin Netanyahu (the current Prime Minister of Israel) and had an interesting experience that involved being in a safe room with both Mr. Sharon and Mr. Netanyahu.

Upon returning stateside in 1991, and after having been involved in three different armed conflicts, Allan's fiancé and eventual wife, Nancy persuaded Allan to change his focus and stay stateside. Wild adventures gone, DEC morphed into a successful database publisher of construction and real estate activity that is still in business today.

Even though that shift represented a major change in his career, Allan was still as productive as ever. Allan was selected by the Atlanta Journal as one of Atlanta's Movers and Shakers and later DEC and the Atlanta Journal co-created the then new Horizon Business Construction/Real Estate section of the paper.

While still excelling in his role at DEC, Allan and Nancy gradually moved to North Florida where they became permanent residents in 2008. Around 2005, Allan began his political career when he was elected President of Concerned Citizens of Franklin County, a Tax Watch Dog group. This role afforded him a myriad of speaking opportunities including the local, state and federal government and even testifying before the Florida House and Senate.

A lifelong Republican, Allan has always been conservative in his views. In light of recent events, Allan felt compelled to write his new book after he and others felt helpless watching the destruction of what was once the undisputed greatest nations on earth.

Made in the USA
Coppell, TX
24 July 2021